FERAL
COUNTRY

.

DAVID MORRIS

Outskirts Press, Inc.
Denver, Colorado

Feral Country

Outskirts Press
http://www.outskirtspress.com

ISBN-10: 1-598000-424-7
ISBN-13: 978-1-59800-424-3

RELATIONSHIPS

A curious breeze breaks
the silence

to ask me
what the hell I'm doing here

why I
why anyone

would ramble around
in a burned up
gray
cracked
bentonite flat
sprinkled
with yellow drooped grasses
withered sage
and the occasional bright white bone

It's simple
I can explain
some men are drawn
to dubious women

the hardest toughest loneliest
country hereabouts
is just naturally attracted
to me.

SOUL FOOD

Rare October Sunday treat:
one hunting season done
the next for several days delayed
means
somebody hungry for a hike
can ramble safely
lead free.

I travel north
and west of Maybell
early out for a bellyful
of red-cliffed country!
Then for dessert
I set my sights
on a sun-simmered hill of white sand
topped with massive globs
of distorted sandstone
like huge pink scoops
of ice cream.

Here's a day
not yet half done
and me already
full to bursting.

A HIGH RIDGE IN THE SHEEPSHEAD BASIN

I know
when I'm not wanted
and I'm no way wanted here:
every how or where I turn
rough blocks of stone
impede my path
brittle pinion limbs
pluck at my clothing
snatch my hat
scratch and tear and shred
my skin
and all the while wild winds
hurl screamed
invective at my head.

So what gives?
Why would this ridge
have such a bone to pick with me?
I feel like some petty prowler
caught with my hand
in Mother Nature's drawers.

CANYON DWELLERS

Small drab
near invisible
by day

frogs greet the evening
with bloated shrieks
that echo off russet canyon walls
like the plaintive bleating
of nervous sheep.

Crazed for attention
frog out shouts frog
in a frantic fevered desire to mate.

Raucous!
And I've heard it all before:
the same collective frenzied din
in every college bar
I ever entered.

A BRIDGE TOO FAR

On my initial visit
to this hidden bend on the Little Snake
gray boards dangling
from a rusted cable
like uneven teeth in a sagging smile
dance in the fast high waters
of early spring

Now
harsh relentless August heat
has forced the stream to mainly flee

and I'm left
without a guess
why some toiler in an era long since gone
connected one hard case sun-bleached desert
to an even sparser drier other desert
with a bridge over a river

where for much
of the long lonesome year
a rabbit could elect
to leap across.

PROGRESS

A large and recent lump
of ruby scat
next to a gray bubble-rock slab
hammers home
what I know already

this is
feral country

roadless
fenceless
ageless

but off to the east
the future is creeping in
like the shadow
of a mechanized bird of prey

development
smudges the distant desert
with oily fingers.

SEDUCTION

After a long lot of sweat
and hot work
I climbed at last
on top of her

imagining
in my eagerness
the myriad of wonders I'd find
concealed beneath her sage skirts

but as I have
so often seen

fantasy and reality
are two too different things

she was just another
sun-bleached
barren
stone strewn mesa.

FIGHT!

Foreheads pressed together
dewlaps flapping
wreathed
in expelled breath
like steam from overheated engines

two raven-black bulls
square off
against a fence framed background
of February blinding white
like the twinned spilled ink
of a Rorschach test.

Thick legs strain
in search of purchase
churn up gouts of freshly fallen snow
in an awkward spastic bovine dance
of leaping! shoving!
de-horned hardcore head butt
hassling!

Some wonder Why
can't we all just get along?
I'd have to say
I'm glad they're mad
each with other

and neither one
at me.

WHAT ARE FRIENDS FOR?

They laugh it up and
shake their heads

they say

Jeez he's
up on Cedar Mountain
again
talking back
at twisted junipers
revisiting cliffs
chasing faded game trails!

they say

Who would have guessed
he'd fall
for a lichen-smeared volcanic blister?

like they have room to talk
good guys
and for the most part

crazier than I am

SPLIT
PERSONALITY

Just as these
half buried broken rocks
went red
long ago altered
by the toasty glow
of Ute cooking fires
so my skin visibly darkens
under the auspices
of an angry summer sun.

The gnarled limbs
of the nearby cedar
provide nothing
in the way of shade
her aged trunk
long since ripped in two
by some vicious
furious wind.

Both splintered halves
of what was once a single she
hold on
to a twisted existence
laying claim
to what could well be
her sister's roots.

SELF-SACRIFICE

Climb high enough
above the desert floor
and you'll see
Little Snake
slither from a crack in Cross Mountain
follow a curvaceous valley course
and rush
headlong
into her bigger sister's side.

Once she
with Yampa becomes one
her sense of self
is gone forever
but she adds that extra
power punch
a river has to have
as she bullies her way
through mile after mile after mile
of hard rock canyon country.

PANIC

Hit the brakes
pass the truck with the orange flag
find yourself sudden
sucked in
to a surging shifting heaving sea
of sheep.
Seems fun at first
like driving through
banks of drifting cloud
and peaceful, too:
multitudinous hooves
bang the pavement
with the musical clatter
of heavy raindrops.

Time passes and
the novelty ebbs
replaced by nervous revelation:
you're an island
hemmed in by frothy waves
of dirty woolly white
your Everywhere
consists of sheep
aimless rudderless sheep
sheep fore and sheep aft
no end of sheep!

You're trapped
in a microcosm
of bleats and bells
the only road forward
with the flow.

FROST

North of nowhere
on a frigid Sunday afternoon

the sky is blue fire
surface crystals spark
like spilled silver sequins.

On a distant fence post
a lone raven rants
in love with the sound
of his own throaty croak

while to my front
two obsolete
eroded roads
diverge
across a bleak wintery expanse
each vying for the title
Road Less Traveled By.

I split the difference

follow neither

let my feet
punching rhythmic
through crusted snow
take the blame
for wherever
I do
or don't
end up.

RED DESERT "G" SPOT

After crossing miles
of sun-seared hard scrabble hills
garnished with prickly pear
and sparse withered grasses
I stumble into a cap rock Camelot:
spires and turrets and castle walls
hemmed in by broken cliffs.

Faded scratches
on cream-colored sandstone
attest to others
who long ago liked it
well enough to stay

but a bilious black mass
gathers to the west

so as for me

I'm leaving.

POWER PLACE

And across the silent
sage-scented valley
bathed in the bright light
of afternoon powder blue sky
a giant's thumb
of red slick rock.
Along it's flank and under
long-term continual construction
three someday arches.

Comforting reassurance!
Wind and heavy weather
carry on
at their own ultra-languid pace
unaffected
by the manic haste
of modern inhumanity.

DEERLODGE

Every mountain hill and ridge
is gift wrapped
in pre-holiday gray
despite a steady soggy snow
only cedars and sage
wear white.

I pause near an edge of jagged cliff
in a bowl of pumpkin-colored sand
where a total lack of wind for once
allows me to think of things
for which I'm thankful

like Mother Yampa far below
hard at work as always and ever
creating canyon country.

IDES OF MARCH IN SAND ROCK COUNTRY

Maybe it's my lucky day:
that super-sized bruised and blacked out
accumulation
of rain and blowing snow

could be headed
toward some other elsewhere--

Fat Chance.

I'd better find some fun fast
among these white stone ramparts:

Normally no future teller
I've read my fortune in the clouds.

EARLY MAY

High on a rocky prow
in a soft and sun-flushed breeze
I sail above an emerald sea
of viridescent rolling hills.
Early May's yearly gift:
a fragrant glut of chlorophyll!

Too soon and sudden
all these variegated shades
of green
will silent slip away
down
the long
gray
drain
of overheated summer.

BROKEN STATUE

Among wind clapped cottonwood branches
in a steep rock strewn ravine
I surprise
a woman's head
cold and white
wedged in a crack of sandstone.

I don't bother wondering
who her rude attacker was
or from what garden
she was topped and taken
no
the thing that gets to me
is how she came to rest in such
a deep and distant place
eyes blank in the Grecian style
dreaming plaster dreams.

BONE YARD

On this grave and humble
greasewood hillside
modified
and redefined
as a home
for retired quadrupeds
absolute equal
reigns:
the newly dead
wrapped in sun-dried hide
mingle freely
with the sprawled
bleached
bones
of the long gone.

Each deceased beast
has a tale
to tell
of succulent grasses
cool water
and the poignant joys
of the occasional rut
but the coarse desert heat
and the passage of time
renders each
and every one
sooner than later
inarticulate.

WILD HORSES

I've got no beef
with feral mustangs
but I'm not wild
about these
Little Snake desert dwellers;
usually aloof
I've seen them mean.

It's their turf not mine
I've tried hard to steer clear
but now the whole gang
gazes my way and
ambles over.

Diomede's horses
back in the BC
were said to be munchers
of human flesh

figuratively speaking
is this bunch coming
to eat
or greet?

GHOST

High up and far away
from the silvered ribbon of river
she's hard at it
scraping a hide
with a sharp-edged flint.

She's glad to be alone glad
to sit in the soft secluded embrace
of a premature spring
where she can listen
to the whispered hum
of the wind.

Sudden as a dropped pot
her mellow mood shatters:

she pulls the hide
protective
to her breast
and vanishes
into a distant past

just as I enter the scene

but I know she was here
I see the stone
she left behind
in a nest of sun-warmed sand.

AFTER A STORM

Unwilling
to accept the final fall of fall
we visited
the valley of the Little Snake
pleasantly surprised to see
recent snows
already beginning to lose their grip:
patches of tan hillside
showing through
a world gone other where winter white.
We prowled
moisture softened sand banks
along the river
gray and crammed
with shards of ice.
A steady breeze walked with us
full of tales
of future heavy weather
of bitter air
poised to pour in
from some far frigid north
but we didn't listen
not on such a magic day
with just the right time
and the perfect place
seamless blended together.

ENCOUNTER

The loud pops
of shattering sticks
perhaps the merest glimpse
of brown:
signs
something's up.
I step out of scrub oak
and in
to the midst
of a plentiful herd of well-dressed elk
ladies in capes
males bowed
beneath the weight
of heavy crowns.

By stopping standing
perfect still
I'm tolerated
ignored by a meandering most
stared at wide-eyed
by a flustered few
but when I choose
to make a move
the whole gang parades
in one long line away.

No skin off my fanny;
not in a party mode
I'm content
with my own company.

WEST OF ELK SPRINGS

I wade
purposeful
into a sea of waist high sage
destined for
a homestead
some mile or more away
the first
of several planned stops
on a Sunday late
October afternoon.

Strange feel indeed
to visit
such a sorry wreck
once warm and tight and dry
now neglected broken sagging saved
from total annihilation
by the rough embrace
of a surround of cottonwoods.
And yet
like some long sunken
fish-infested ship
here's an abode
awash
in birds rabbits wood chucks mice
ants spiders wasps flies
living proof
no house is ever
not
a home.

REVELATION

Deep in the darkest
alcove canyon cracks
we inspected the rock-walled remnants
of a culture long gone
and wondered
what chased those folks
in ancient days away.
Meticulous builders!
Were they driven off by drought?
Worn down by warfare?
Crushed
by the weight
of their own too many?
Maybe.
But.
I heard an aged ghost
who whispered this:

We vanished, yes.
We'd had it!
Up to here!
With god damned ravens!
No rest for us
no peace,
not with that late
and all night noisy
cacophony of croaks!
Show offs--
they spent the daylight
barrel rolling black
against a sky electric blue
as if they owned the place.

[27]

MEDICINE WHEEL

Whoever they were they
long ago chose
a superior spot
to worship something
or someone
or maybe different things
at different times:
a grassy open place
on an otherwise cedar-covered thumb
entrance to a stream-cut canyon
on one side
miles of red-boulder high ground
on the other.

LATE MARCH

This hillside
is a huge womb
a big brown belly
soft sun-warmed
soggy with snow melt:
too much at the moment
of a good thing.
Nothing green
but another week or two
of days like this one
and the life crouched
just beneath the surface
will bust up and burst out
salute the sky
and take a bow
to April.

TWILIGHT SONG

Make a song. Sing
the benevolence of the White Man's Way!
He gifts us with a sea of beads
asks in return only
our lands and sacred places.

Sing the charitability of the White Man!
He presses upon us
his god
whose son died for the evil we do
asks in return nothing
but the rubbing out of a way of seeing
a way of being
a way of life.

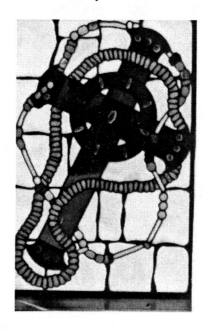

BUFFALO SKULL

We met in the depths
of a crack in the earth--
he'd rest there still
had my eyes not seized upon
horn and the merest bit of bone;
a nearly buried treasure
stark white against the chocolate brown
of a vertical wall.
I groveled blissful in the dirt
to make this prize my own;
Like some galvanized savage I
chipped furious away with tools of stone
until I finally dragged him free, free at last
from ancient grave and
hard clay's cool embrace!

RAIN

The sky is a patchwork quilt
of shades of gray
a gray that hints at maybe rain
good-natured shift
from the drab and ominous veil
of wildfire smoke
we've lately had to learn
to live with.

Air cools
droplets slap bone dry sand
with the sound of polite applause.
Better look sharp
huddle up under a cedar fast
one that offers
some shred of sanctuary:
that deep belly-rumbling roar
can only mean
a wind-driven wall of frenzied weather.

Sun soon signals the all clear
but don't move!
Stay still!
Drink up
the short-lived musty minty smell
of wet sage and rain-trampled grasses
and the loud silence
of a world gone
for merest moment
mute.

PRIVATE PROPERTY

A lone raven
fat and sleek black
shivers the January mid day silence
with his raucous monotone
croak.
He's raising the alarm
and rightly so;
printed warnings
several too many to ignore
have made it as abundant clear
as the frigid air
I'm not supposed
to trespass here.
Still the snow is deep
and sweet for skiing
and I'm the only
anyone
anywhere around
so I guess I'll what the hell
take my time
take my chances.

WEST OF LAY

Like a drone drawn
to a distant broken blossom
I can't resist
an ancient pick up
hunkered down in the midst of nowhere
hood raised
in a permanent smile
tires gone
axles deep in decades
of wind-driven sand.
A midden pile lies hidden
in a drywash nearby.
Enameled pots and pans
nestle like ripe fruits
among the usual assortment
of bones bottles rusted tin:
prizes I careful pluck.

Not until I've traveled
a good ways off
do I see the reason
for truck and trash--
gray as November sage
near invisible
overpowered by passing years
the remains of a homestead
hug a hillside:
a site that once shined with life
forever to the limelight
lost.

NORTH PARK

Rain
gave up
moved on
driven off by a July
of searing ultra warm
leaving the land to whiten and die.
To the west
lines of angry buttes
defy the summer sun;
brutish purple flattened fists,
they tower
in the evening heat
and punch
the bloodied sky.

EAGLE TRAP

Once upon an ancient early dawn
a man emerged from a cluster of boulders
moved up a hogback to red cliff's edge
Thirsty work.

Crouched inside a circle
of waist high stacked rock
he made a dead rabbit dance
spent his day fishing the sky for eagles.

A trapping place
already old in his day.
He came upon it in his wanderings
as I have in mine.

HIGHWAY 40

Far to the west I discover
a long stretch
of the old road
Victory Way
named for the War
to End All Wars.
Wars never got around
to ending but
this highway did--
tight curves and roller coaster climbs
were in the sixties sliced away
like coils of ancient snake
by tractors and graders
strong enough to gouge and bully
a flatter straighter route.
Little is left:
macadam turned to gravel
gravel to sand
windblown
blasted.
A new road now runs slick
efficient level fast;
this old route
would have made for slow going
travelers forced to take the time
to know the road they traveled.

ABANDONED SHEEP RANCH

We step gingerly
into cool rank dark
having to guess
at first
what it is we're seeing
with our unadjusted eyes:
a room decorated
with the shriveled paws of coyotes
nailed up like detached tiny hands
in lines along the cross beams
in geometric patterns
across graying clapboard walls.
Hundreds of paws
too many to begin to count:
a patterned display
of long dead things
in an equally dead
ancient abandoned
wind-pounded dry-rotted
bunkhouse
miles down a lonely country road
somewhere deep in the Red Desert.

ONE SUNDAY IN THE RED DESERT

A dirt road
slick rutted potholed steep.
It may not look like much
(other than a thing upon which
we should never be driving
on a cold wet late fall day like this)
but what a fortuitous finest find!
It's a passage to high and higher still
through stands of ancient cedars
sculptured rock.
Humble road
seldom used
it gives the gift of distant vistas:
plum colored mesas and
row upon row of reddish buttes
like stolid squatting birds
nested in sodden wisps
of broken cloud.

BEYOND QUIET

I tell myself
Stand still awhile

Listen hard and could be hear

the soft anguished sigh
of snow melting

the scratch and pop of gnarled roots
stretching awake
in cool wet ground

the sound of water fed grasses fattening

the quiet hiss of high gray tinged clouds
sliding in from the west

all that and more to listen for
yet I must ruin
an almost perfect silence
with the sodden sucking sounds
of my own footsteps

too ADD
to stay stopped
long enough to really listen
to any one
place or thing.

CROSS MOUNTAIN

Up among cedars and coffee colored chunks
of lava rock
I snap up that first chip
of the morning
study its opaque pearl-ness
feel it's hard, sharp edges nip
at my finger tips.

It's Sunday a.m., and
the wind is sleeping in;
sun, though, is up-- and
after last week's first cold and snow
it makes a strong showing,
dousing me with golden heat
like stove-warmed syrup.
Distant hillsides
flame with leafy orange and red
Steller's Jays, exuberant, shriek

and I stagger on my merry way
buzzed up and near delirious drunk
on a bellyful of fall.

DUMP

Yeah, I know,
I've seen it too many times before but
still I stop, still sigh,
ask myself

What is this mess doing here?

I take a somber stroll
through sand and sage corrupted:

one washing machine drum, rusted out
gnarled wire, some barbed, some not
the inevitable ancient bed spring
corrugated tin
gray rotted boards
bones assorted
tires, bald
oxidized bolts, nails
broken bottles, white blue brown clear and
cans cans cans cans cans cans cans cans.

A mourning dove flushes
wings away;
I don't blame her.
I'd fly too
from me and my kind.

CEMETERY

There would have been no where to run
even if somehow
they'd been able to run.
How they must have trembled
when first they felt
death coming:
ancient cedars
engulfed like anchored squid
by a tidal wave of furious flame
here in the very canyon where
unmolested
they'd passed so many quiet centuries.

They stand here still
by the hundred hundreds:
naked contorted limbs
scorched a glistening black
reach for clouds
with empty lifeless hands.

SPRING STORM

I never thought I could think
believed I could see
this world, my world
through the eyes of a chicken
but tonight the sky is falling
the darkness filled
with white acorns.

TRADE BEADS

Now look
what you've done a mother
must have chided.
I asked you
not to play with that didn't I
ask you
not to play with that?
Your father traded soft furs
for that fine necklace.
Now look.

Beaded necklace broken:
pearls of glass
cobalt blue turquoise green
spilled out on sandy soil.
The child no doubt tried
retrieval
but never could reclaim them all
no child could.

Left to drift some hundred years
in sifting sand
they seem to choose to reappear:
trade beads
stirred by warm spring winds
surfacing like colored snails.

GRAVE SITE

A child's grave--
No way what
I expected to find
high above a Yampa
horseshoe turn
on a slate gray day;
but then the one buried
could well be
equally surprised by my arrival.

Reticent headstone!
1902-1905 the plain and only
data supplied
besides the name the youngster bore
faded long ago away
like the people who here planted
their short-lived seed.

Lonely, sure
but there are worse places
for even an infant
to spend forever:
red rocks take the place
of a mother's encircling arms
distant geese
yammer like excited dogs
and the view from the bluff
is hard to beat.
Yes I could live with this
When I am someday dead.

MAIL ORDER BRIDE

Honey he says
we're here
this is it
and account of we're man and wife
he says
all yours now as well as mine
like I'm a going to jump for joy
over a few hundred acres
of bone dry sage-covered clay hills
Jesus!
No house yet he says
we got to make a go of things first
he's done scraped a cave
out of a hillside
rocked the front up
I got to live
like some stooped over troglodyte
with a man I won't ever forgive
and nobody nowhere to talk at
except a wind that talks so much itself
it don't often bother to listen.

GEESE

Far below in the shadowed bottoms
of a river-notched passage
riders on the Little Snake
hear or feel my presence
one hundred feet at least above them
where I've ventured near
the canyon's lichen spattered lip.
Their fierce and frantic echoed screams
catch me way off guard
in such a blank and empty place.
Not until in a bunch they spring
up and out and further off
in a flurry of furious wing beats
do I know whose feathers
my arrival
have so badly ruffled.

THE GREAT DIVIDE

Like a belled cat I
disturb the midmorning quiet:
keys coins bits of stone
rut and clang in the loose
pockets of my shorts
like hornets stirred up
by my lurching gait.
The noise I make works
to wake the dead;
I am surrounded by silent spirits
desert dwellers long since shoved aside
by my own ambitious kind.

SOMETHING FISHY NORTH OF BAGGS

A plethora of shellfish
in a barren uplifted plain
seems as woefully out of place
as pearls in a pauper's ring.
Fact: any water pooled here
was eons earlier
chased from the scene;
all forms of moisture since have shunned
this burned and baked locale.

Okay, but check out these rocks:
straight from the bottom
of a long gone shallow inland sea
they're packed with the remains
of used to be life.

Millions of hours have passed away
since these sea creatures
crawled to quiet death;
they lacked the gift
to know or see
their own future
reappearance and immortality
in stone.

SKIING ON THIN ICE

I tear along
this river race track
nearly skating
skis hissing
on an inch of fresh white satin.
Fear enlivens pace:
I can hear and feel
the pulse of the current
frantic heartbeat
beneath fragile fabric
of snow and ice and
ten feet to my left
blue waters have broken free
to hammer at crusty borders
with fists of foam.
What's on today's menu?
Snow, cold, speed, danger--
a meal of pure exhilaration!

WRONG PLACE WRONG TIME RED DESERT

The day is dark
and difficult to get along with;
manic winds race wild about
like spoiled, frigid children.
Snow showers, I'd guessed
were a done deal--
time to guess again!
Pelted by first flurries
I turn and inward cringe
dismayed by the rapid advance
of a wall of raging gray.
It's almost May, I tell myself, it
wouldn't white out on me . . .
would it?

I begin a rapid uphill haul
thinking I know which way to go
but how can I be sure
when one by one my landmarks disappear
erased in a gale of furious white?
A rush of fear
whispers: You're lost
you're alone
and a long blind way from nowhere.

Nothing much ever changes in this country:
I picture some other nomadic male
here, on a day just like today
a hundred, a thousand, five thousand
years ago.
Caught in an angry cloud he
tugs a blanket tight
across frozen shoulders
and mumbles to himself,
Don't you just hate it
when this happens?

SURPRISE!

I'm high on the side
of a barren butte
and in a hurry.
Like a hyper flea
I bound down a massive bentonite back
choose to scoot around
a heap of rocks by nature piled:
lucky, happy choice!
Tipped off by a furious frenzied buzz
I turn to see a mass of glistening coils
thicker than a big man's wrist,
a scaly fanged fortress
into the midst of which I've near intruded.

I know when to dodge a bad scene;
so does a lime green riled rattler.
With astounding speed (for a serpent her age)
she slithers below ground, gone
to celebrate her safety
with an adamant shake of the tail.
I move off with pounding heart
my tail shaking too.

CHANGING SEASON

I crest the hill and there's
Black Mountain rearing up
giant head
covered with hair of pine and spruce.
But hey, what's with
that sorry case of dandruff?
Makes my own scalp prickle and itch!
Okay, I can't deny
mountain peaks look sparkling best
hatted with cream stetsons but
Summer and I had one hell of a time--
I'd hold him by his coattails
if I could
to keep him from leaving.

TICK

As I shower off the dust
of a dry desert morning,
my soaped fingers hesitate
over a foreign something.
Damn.
No need to see it to see it:
He's chocolate brown flat-shelled
stealthy and
caught in his act--
living it up
anchored in the dark moist
of my armpit.
I'd guess there were
a multitude of hosts
out in the sandy sage-clothed hills
he could have joined for lunch
but he chose me.
Unflattered
I pinch him off.
This is my body, my blood;
I can't provide
for every hungry stray
in search of a free meal.

100 ANTELOPE SELF-DESTRUCT ON A BLUFF ABOVE THE GREEN RIVER

A white velvet curtain
dropped down, hung around
decided to stay over
this pronghorn party.
Like some atmospheric Pied Piper
the cloud clouded antelope judgment;
they didn't just kick
back, lay low, let
the foggy trickster
lift, leave, lean
into other desert canyons.
No, they had to follow
the call of some silent flute
blinded, even with eyes
the size of brown silver dollars.
They formed a ruminant conga line,
face to tail to tail to face
danced with mincing steps
over a hundred foot cliff.

VERMILION CREEK PETROGLYPHS

That's my old man up there
perched like some over-eager woodpecker
on a narrow crumbling ledge
hammering away at hard red rock.
My friends, they're all blessed
with run-of-the-mill dads:
hunters, flint shapers,
killers of our enemies.
Me? I'm saddled with a pop
who squanders every sun-drenched hour
tapping dreams
into red canyon walls.

DESERT LOVE

Down and dirty on the desert's floor
an ebony something
glitters like obsidian--it
isn't.
Two beetles wrestle and writhe
in the throes of must be bug ecstasy;
closer inspection
does not embarrass or disturb,
absorbed as they are
in awkward, piggyback procreation.
Hot light
caroms off hard, black shells;
finally Easter!

EAGLE

Lazily aloof, the raptor king
coasts into sight;
his streamlined glide
perks me up like fresh brewed!
Some wings! Spread
as if to shield
the sun from the earth
each pinion tipped
in wizard-beard white.
He's got
a head of polished ivory and
attached to that
a Caesar's beak.

He banks, soars in low,
drops to the two track,
feathers flaring
as if to wave away
dinner guests uninvited.

He tears himself a magenta chunk
of bunny gut well seasoned,
tenderized by Good Year rubber
and bolts it,
while I digest the fact
even the gods eat garbage.

EVENING SKI

With each rhythmic lunge
my narrow skis
slap along in crusted grooves
past cottonwoods
drooped under heavy white gowns
like a convention
of stunned and jilted brides.
To my left
the river, roped in ice,
cries out its garbled freedom pleas
where fast currents
force away the icy gag.
Darkness tiptoes in;
psychotic nurse, she
smothers her patient, End of Day
with a black satin pillow.

FALL IN NORTHWEST COLORADO

Well, it might have been
the scrub oak—
it made the whole hillside bloody
under early morning sun
or the eagles
swarming like bees
above that once was a rabbit
as I zipped past
or those Sand Hill cranes
splashed across a September sky.
In any case some
thing or things
made me too aware
of warm heater purr and
shoulder belt pressure
like a gentle caress across my chest:
there I was
rattling down a dirt road
storm clouds of brown dust
in my wake
declaring
my undying love
to a pickup truck.

HOT TIMES IN MID-JULY

Today the desert is a suffering giant
exhaling fevered breath.
My charbroiled feet suck the heat
from a cracked and blistered skin.
The oven that old witch readied for Gretel
(for herself, it turns out)
has nothing over this ground!
Bentonite, they tell me,
clay, anyway, and sand,
baked like a Shoshone pot
gray and red, no glaze.
Unlike Hansel, I'm not lost,
and it's a good thing, too:
canteen half empty
water warm to the touch
like the blood of an Englishman.

AFTER A RAIN IN LADORE CANYON

The sky has emptied itself
at least for now;
a cloud bank hangs
on the canyon's crimson walls
exhausted, soggy, cried out.
Like an obsessive lover
it clings to cold cliffs
afraid of being pushed away
to dissipate alone somewhere
over barren indifferent desert.

A HIKE IN THE CORNER OF THE RED DESERT

Ye gods! If God
did indeed fashion
the Heavens and the Earth,
She was in a pestilential foulest mood
When put to work on these poor acres!
This ground was ground
beneath the divine heel
until it must have mercy cried
in red and purple agony!
I picture
(in my merely mortal mind)
a creation story:
clay divots fly, boulders roll,
the very air is scorched
by misdirected holy wrath
as prairie hills which might have been
are clubbed into a state that makes
your run-of-the-mill badlands
look good.
To top it off, She hangs the sun
above like some crazed pilot light
to keep this bentonite furnace stoked.
Here little grows and nothing moves
save at the moment me
and whispering snakes of sand.

LAST GASP OF INDIAN SUMMER

There's a power and an attraction in rock
so I'm not surprised
to find me here
atop a long spine
of titanic lichened-spotted sandstone slabs
contemplating
a vast library
of book cliffs.

I wonder
after all these rapid
passing years
has the desert grown on me
or have I grown
on the desert?

DAZE END

Ms. Yampa's on the run
she tears around
an ice-edged white-walled bend
robed in the burnished gold
and turquoise blue
she's stolen from a day
hanging
on the cusp of done

and for a little moment
the churning foggy flow
of my chaotic thought
gets that focused feel

there's a clarity
in the hard cruel cold
of a late December afternoon.

Printed in the United States
49582LVS00002B/418-492